Scho

Who Teaches The Teacher?

Two minute devotions for the busy teacher

Katie Everly

My first year of teaching a coworker told me to write down the weird things you hear at school. I found that strange until I began hearing those strange things you only hear at school. I always thought that someone could write a book just with those weird things! A few years ago I felt this tug on my heart to write a book using those sayings, so I began writing some of them down. Then I felt that I needed to make them into a devotional book for teachers. I'm thinking how do you make "you are not a dinosaur" into a devotion. So I put it on the back burner for a while. That feeling never really went away, so I finally decided to bite the bullet and go for it.

I have written this mostly for teachers, but anyone who has been around kids could also enjoy it. There are 45 days to coincide with a full marking period for teachers. I hope this brings you a laugh and a sense of peace and purpose each day. I pray that God blesses you!

Special Thanks to:

Nikki, Sam, and Lisa who helped me with ideas when I was having writer's block! Thanks to all the teachers I've worked with over the years.

Day 1

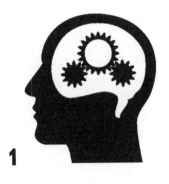

"What did I say to do with your head?"

I remember hearing another teacher say this once without context. It caught my attention! Is the child sleeping? What is that student actually doing with his/her head to cause this question to be asked? I was definitely thinking literally, but I want to think a little deeper now.

*Proverbs 3:13 - **Blessed is the man who finds wisdom, the man who gains understanding***

*Proverbs 16:16 - **How much better to get wisdom than gold, to choose understanding rather than silver!***

Wisdom is the ability to make good judgements based on your knowledge. Understanding is the ability to grasp your own knowledge and choices. The writer of these Proverbs specifically says that you are blessed if you have wisdom and understanding; also that it is better than silver or gold!

How do we get them? You can acquire and develop both through experience. When you make a mistake, learn from it. Be thoughtful of others and the experiences they've had. Truly care for others. Wisdom and understanding are things that we are constantly improving on in our Christian walk.

What should we be doing with our heads? Filling it with wisdom and understanding of course!

Dear Lord, Please help me to gain wisdom and understanding in a way that can only come from you. Help me model good judgement for my students. Amen

Day 2

"Where's your hand?"

Students do strange things with their hands. Sometimes they wave them around in the air, put them in their pants, put them in their socks, and many other things. Many times they don't even realize they are doing it, until someone asks them what they are doing.

1 Corinthians 12:14-27 is comparing body parts to jobs done in the church

Verses 19-21 "If they were all one part, where would the body be? As it is, there are many parts, but one body. The eye cannot say to the hand, 'I don't need you!' And the head cannot say to the feet, 'I don't need you!'"

Can you imagine what the world would be like if some people were only eyeballs? They would be rolling down the street, just watching. Or what if some people were only hands; just waving. You get the picture. Our bodies have different parts each designed to do different and unique things. Our feet are made for walking, running, jumping. Our eyes are made to see. Our hands are made for touching things, writing things, holding things, etc. Now some people have been able to train different body parts to do even more unique things; such as someone with no arms using their feet to drive and pick things up. The main point is that God made us with different body parts for different purposes.

It is the same way with the body of Christ, the church. If everyone preaches, there will be no one to listen. If everyone sings, there would be no one to play instruments.

Verse 27 – Now you are the body of Christ, and each one of you is a part of it.

If everyone did the same thing, life would be very boring indeed. God gifted us all with unique and special gifts that we should be using for His glory.

So "Where's your hand?" Hopefully it's being used in the way God made it!

Dear Lord, Help me to do the job you created me to do. Teach me to use my hand in the correct way and not compare what I'm doing to anyone else. Amen

Day 3

No, I don't want to smell your hand

The funniest part of this statement is that it has been said more times than I can remember. Kids ask me to smell their hands many times in a year. Most of the time it is after they've used hand sanitizer, lotion, or washed their hands. Unfortunately, sometimes it's not. Due to not knowing what it is I will be smelling, I usually decline to smell their hands.

2 Corinthians 2:15-16 For we are to God the aroma of Christ among those who are being saved and those who are perishing. To the one we are the smell of death; to the other, the fragrance of life. And who is equal to such a task?

The Bible is full of references to things with fragrance. This specific set of verses says we are an aroma to God. When we are living for Christ and showing our Christian testimony to others it is a sweet fragrance of life to God. However, others may see it as the smell of death. When we show God's love to others, we show them how sweet the love of God is. We cannot have control over how others will receive our testimony (whether they will think it smells sweet or like death), but it is our responsibility to show them the love of God.

People may respond by not wanting to smell your hand, but that doesn't mean you stop showing them love.

Dear God, Help me show others your love and share my testimony with them, no matter how they might respond. Let them see God's love in me and know that it is a sweet fragrance. Amen

Day 4

Go wash your hands

Keep your hands to yourself

Hands are a very important part of your body. Most elementary students need reminders to wash their hands. The littler kids need reminders to keep their hands to themselves. And sometimes you get asked to smell someone's hands. As you can see a lot of things are said to students about hands. Which is interesting to me because the Bible also has many references to hands.

Psalm 37:24 - though he stumble, he will not fall, for the Lord upholds him with his hand.

Psalm 139:10 - even there your hand will guide me, your right hand will hold me fast.

John 10:28-29 - I give them eternal life, and they shall never perish; no one can snatch them out of my hand. My Father, who has given them to me, is greater than all; no one can snatch them out of my Father's hand.

These verses are a few of many that talk about the hand of God. The first two about how God will hold us and guide us. The last one is Jesus speaking about people who believe in him. Jesus says if we believe in him, he has given us eternal life. We will not perish because no one can take us out of his hand nor the Father's hand. This verse has given me such peace in life. Jesus said no one can take us out of his hand. There isn't anything that anyone can do that can steal our eternal salvation. Once you are a child of God, you are always a child of God.

So when you wash your hands, remember that you are always in your Father's hands.

Dear Heavenly Father, Thank you for keeping me in your hand. I can know for certainty that once I believe in you no one can take me out of your hand. I am always and forever your child. Amen

Day 5

"Mute your mic!"

This is a relatively new phrase that a lot of teachers have had to begin using. As I am writing this during a pandemic; teachers have had to transition to online learning. For many this includes virtual meetings. I've had to teach my students how to mute their mics, so we can actually hear the person who is talking.

*James 1:19 - **My dear brothers, take note of this: Everyone should be quick to listen, slow to speak and slow to become angry.***

The kids are so excited to see their friends and classmates that they just want to talk all at the same time. Of course, then you can't hear anyone. When they learn to take turns and listen to one another first, that's when they can have real conversations.

Isn't that true in life also? If we learn to listen to what other people say first, instead of thinking about how we will respond, we can have much better conversations. First listen and understand what others are saying; being slow to speak or respond. Process before speaking and then you will be less likely to become angry.

Remember to "mute your mic" before you speak!

Dear God, Please help me to "mute my mic" before responding. Help me to fully listen when someone is speaking and understand what they are saying before responding. Amen

Day 6

"Thoughts stay inside your head. They don't come out of your mouth"

Children have a tendency to blurt. They just say whatever pops into their head. Our thoughts have a huge impact on what comes out of our mouths. As adults, we have a little more control over our thoughts than kids do; but we still struggle.

Psalm 19:14 - May the words of my mouth and the meditation of my heart be pleasing in your sight, O Lord, my Rock and my Redeemer.

Proverbs 18:21a - The tongue has the power of life and death

These verses serve as a good reminder that what is in our heads and hearts will eventually come out in our actions or words. Our words have tremendous power over ourselves and over others. We have to be careful that what we are thinking is positive and pleasing to God. Then what comes out in our words and actions will also be positive and pleasing to God.

Think before you talk. Not everything you think needs to come out of your mouth. Be positive and speak life.

Dear Lord, Help me to use my words in a positive way. Let my thoughts, words and actions be pleasing to you. Amen

Day 7

Stop talking

Kids love to talk: to each other, to the teacher, and sometimes to themselves. This means that kids need a reminder to stop talking on occasion. It can be in the hallways, during a fire drill, during instruction, and many other times.

Job 37:14 - Listen to this, Job; stop and consider God's wonders.

Sometimes we need to stop and focus on the wonders of God. Job was reminded of this and we are also. Look around at the wonders and mysteries of God. Focus and think on the amazing things God has done. Nature itself holds so many incredible sights that God created for us to enjoy.

Rainbows, clouds, storms, flowers, the breeze, the ocean, this list could go on forever!

Also, so many sounds for us to enjoy: birds, crickets, frogs, thunder, voices, etc.

God reminds us to just stop. If we look around and marvel at his creation, we will have a more positive outlook on everything.

God created so much for us to enjoy. We need to stop talking and just focus on Him.

Dear God, Thank you for all that you created for me to enjoy. Help me to stop and focus on you. Amen

Day 8

Stop making noises!

If you have ever worked with children then you know that they are noisy. Talking, yelling, bodily noises, tapping, sometimes just noises that they don't even realize they are making. And almost always this occurs at the most inopportune times. It is the meaningless noise that can become quickly irritating. The noise that comes from students talking through problems, working in small groups, reading together, etc. is wonderful.

Psalm 100:1 (ESV) - Make a joyful noise to the Lord all the earth!

Noises can be a beautiful thing. If you can sing, then sing. If you can play an instrument, then play your instrument. If you are a good speaker, then speak. Use the noises you are good at making for God's glory. We can use our noises/voices for a variety of things. What we need to consider is how we can bring God the glory. We can choose to argue, use bad language, be condescending, be rude, etc. Or we can choose to be kind, use loving words and tones, be respectful to one another, praise God, tell others about God, etc.

Use your noise/voice in such a way that God never thinks "Stop making noises!"

Dear God, Help me to use my voice in the way you want me to. Help me to make a joyful noise for you, that others will know you by what I say and how I say it. Amen

Day 9

Why am I hearing voices?

I work in an open space school, so sometimes I hear voices that are not even coming from my classroom. It can make me feel a little crazy sometimes! I ask my class why I can still hear their voices, but as I look around I realize it's not even coming from them (except for the times that it does come from them).

Romans 10:17-18 - Consequently, faith comes from hearing the message, and the message is heard through the word of Christ. But I ask: Did they not hear? Of course they did: "Their voice has gone out into all the earth, their words to the ends of the world."

What are we using our voices for? As Christians, our goal should be that everyone knows the Good News of Christ. Our voices should be used for Christ. Tell others about God when you can and use your voice to show the love of God to everyone. People should hear your voice loving others the way God would. We need to use our voices to show respect to others too. How will others have faith if they don't hear about God?

Why am I hearing voices? Hopefully it's because we are spreading God's love to others!

Dear God, Help me to use my voice to tell others about You. Also help me use my voice to show love and respect to others. Amen

Day 10

"Thank you for putting your peace sign up"

The school where I teach uses peace signs to remind students when it is time to be quiet. We also recognize one student from each classroom each month as a Peacebuilder of the Month. Peace can sometimes mean quiet and sometimes it means showing kindness and gentleness in who you are.

John 14:27 – "Peace I leave with you; my peace I give you. I do not give to you as the world gives. Do not let your hearts be troubled and do not be afraid."

Jesus is speaking these words to His disciples when He is forewarning them about His death and resurrection. He is giving them and us peace, which is greater than anything that may trouble you or make you afraid!

John 16:33 – I have told you these things, so that in me you may have peace. In this world you will have trouble. But take heart! I have overcome the world."

Jesus is once again speaking these words. He doesn't tell us we might have some trouble. He says we WILL have trouble. This is when we need to remember that God has given us peace.

Anytime we have trouble; we also have God's peace which is greater than any trouble we will have.

Philippians 4:6-7 – *"Do not be anxious about anything, but in everything, by prayer and petition, with thanksgiving, present your requests to God. And the peace of God, which transcends all understanding, will guard your hearts and your minds in Christ Jesus."*

Anxiety is something that plagues a lot of people and I am by no means an expert. However, God does give us some advice in dealing with anxiety. When you feel anxious, remember to pray and ask God for peace. He will give us peace, sometimes we just need to ask.

Remember to put your peace sign up to remember to quiet your soul. And be a peacebuilder and remind others to look to God for peace.

Lord, Please give me peace in my soul today and everyday. Calm and quiet my soul, so I can be a calming influence on my students. Amen

Day 11

"Change your color"

At my school and many other schools, students have a color system for their behavior. Ours in particular uses the colors blue, green, yellow and red. Blue and green being good, yellow means a warning and red is pretty bad. I've told my kids before it's like a stop light: green means keep doing what you are doing, yellow means slow down and think about what you've been doing, and red means you better stop! (Blue is when they go above and beyond expectations).

There are many references to colors in the bible. The color green typically symbolizes growth in life and in the Christian faith. Green is good - God wants us to be growing! Blue reminds us of the sky, which may also trigger thoughts of Heaven. Heaven is our ultimate goal, just as blue in school should be a child's ultimate goal. Yellow is often used in place of the color gold. Gold represents God's deity and divinity. It can be used as a reminder to us that we need Jesus in our lives. Red is most often used symbolically for the blood of Jesus. Red is a reminder to us that we have all messed up and need the blood of Jesus. We need to stop and acknowledge that.

When we see a color system at school let it remind us:

Blue - Heaven - our ultimate goal

Green - keep growing

Yellow - slow down and remember Jesus is God

Red - we have made mistakes and need the blood of Jesus to help us reach our ultimate goal

Dear God, When I look at colors today and every day, let them remind me of you. Help me to keep growing and remember that Jesus is God! Amen

Day 12

Effort

I am constantly explaining to my classes that they need to display effort in their work. That I don't expect everything they do to be perfect, but I do expect them to put forth effort and try their best. It is a constant ebb and flow of effort throughout the school year. It is something that I really push and ask my students to strive to put forth their best effort always.

2 Peter 1:5-8 – For this reason, make every effort to add to your faith goodness; and to goodness knowledge; and to knowledge, self-control; and to self-control, perseverance; and to perseverance, godliness; and to godliness, brotherly kindness; and to brotherly kindness, love. For if you possess these qualities in increasing measure, they will keep you from being ineffective and unproductive in your knowledge of our Lord Jesus Christ.

Simon Peter gives us the same charge. He says to make every effort. Does this mean we are going to do these things perfectly every time? No. But we should be striving to put forth our best effort always. First, we need faith; nothing else on this list even matters without it. Then goodness, knowledge, self-control, perseverance, godliness, brotherly kindness, and finally love are the things Peter tells us to make an effort to do. If we strive to work on these things we will not be ineffective for Jesus. And isn't that what we all want to be considered effective for Jesus!

Put forth the effort and you will be effective!

Dear Lord, Help me to be effective for you. Remind me that I need faith, goodness, knowledge, self-control, perseverance, godliness, kindness, and love. Amen

Day 13

Tests/Grades – Why is it that kids always want to know if an assignment's going to be graded before they begin it? I always ask them why it matters. I explain that they need to do their best either way. The worst kind of grades are pass/fail grades. Thankfully that usually doesn't happen until you are in college and even then it's implemented in very few classes. Tests show what you know and what you lack. The only way to tell if you know something is through some type of testing.

2 Corinthians 13:5-7 – Examine yourselves to see whether you are in the faith; test yourselves. Do you not realize that Christ Jesus is in you – unless, of course, you fail the test? And I trust that you will discover that we have not failed the test. Now we pray to God that you will not do anything wrong – not so that people will see that we have stood the test but so that you will do what is right even though we may seem to have failed.

Paul tells us to test ourselves. To do this we have to examine our hearts. We need to find out if we are in the faith. It will show what we have and what we lack. We can discover this by looking at what comes out of our minds and what comes out of our mouths. The test Paul talks of is a pass/fail test. You are either showing people you have Jesus living in you or you fail.

I pray that everyone reading this passes this test and that you show everyone that you are a child of God.

Dear God, Help me to test myself and know that I have Jesus living in me. Help me to show that in all I do. Amen

Day 14

Checklists – another tool for assessment. As a teacher, you can take a checklist and watch students to determine if they have mastered a certain skill. Checklists are very informal and non-threatening to children. There is a checklist of sorts in the bible also – it consists of two lists – right and wrong.

Galatians 5:19-26 – The acts of the flesh are obvious: sexual immorality, impurity and debauchery; idolatry and witchcraft; hatred, discord, jealousy, fits of rage, selfish ambition, dissensions, factions and envy; drunkenness, orgies, and the like. I warn you, as I did before, that those who live like this will not inherit the kingdom of God. But the fruit of the Spirit is love, joy, peace, forbearance, kindness, goodness, faithfulness, gentleness and self-control. Against such things there is no law. Those who belong to Christ Jesus have crucified the flesh with its passions and desires. Since we live by the Spirit, let us keep in step with the Spirit. Let us not become conceited, provoking and envying each other.

The only way you can tell if something is real or that you have truly learned something is to test it. These two lists are checklists to see if you have a real relationship with God. Obviously, everyone who has a relationship with God makes mistakes and slip-ups every once in a while. The meaning here is that you are not living in the acts of the flesh. That you are doing all you can leaning on

God to live with the fruits of the Spirit. People will know we are God's children if we show them the fruits of the Spirit.

Test yourself with these lists and see how you are doing in walking in the Spirit.

Dear God. Help me to pass the test of walking in the Spirit with the fruits of the Spirit: love, joy, peace, forbearance, kindness, goodness, faithfulness, gentleness, and self-control. Amen

Day 15

"You're not a dinosaur!"

I once said this when a child jumped up on his chair and pretended to be a dinosaur. As much as I appreciated his imagination, during small group reading instruction is just not the appropriate time to be a dinosaur.

There has always been a debate as to if and when dinosaurs even existed. Children have always been obsessed with dinosaurs.

Job 40:15-24 – "Look at the Behemoth, which I made along with you and which feeds on grass like an ox. What strength it has in its loins, what power in the muscles of its belly! Its tail sways like a cedar; the sinews of its thighs are close-knit. Its bones are tubes of bronze, its limbs like rods of iron. It ranks first among the works of God, yet its Maker can approach it with his sword. The hills bring it their produce, and all the wild animals play nearby. Under the lotus plants it lies, hidden among the reeds in the marsh. The lotuses conceal it in their shadow; the poplars by the stream surround it. A raging river does not alarm it; it is secure, though the Jordan should surge against its mouth. Can anyone capture it by the eyes, or trap it and pierce its nose?"

Dinosaur or elephant?? I will let you decide!

Lord, Help me to appreciate and encourage my students' imaginations. Let me continue dreaming also. Amen

Day 16

"You are not a frog"

Kids like to imagine. They like to pretend and play. There are plenty of times for them to do that. While I'm trying to teach is not the time to hop like a frog. When working with little children especially this is bound to happen at least once or twice in your teaching career. Hence the "You are not a frog" comment.

Many times we focus on what we are not and what we are lacking. We are not pretty enough, smart enough, etc. Instead of always focusing on what we are not; we need to be focusing on what we are.

John 1:12 - Yet to all who received him, to those who believed in his name, he gave the right to become children of God

If you have accepted Jesus as your Savior by believing in Him, you are a child of God. That is your right! It doesn't matter what we think we are not, what we think we lack, what others tell us we cannot do; the truth is that we are children of God! He is greater than anything we face or anything we hear. He is bigger than any fear we have! And we are His children!

Don't think that you are a frog! Know that you are a child of God!

Dear God, Thank you for allowing me to be your child. Help me to focus on what I am and not dwell on what I lack. Help me to also see what my students are and not dwell on what they lack. Amen

Day 17

Nature stays outside.

I had a wonderful student (twice actually) who loved nature! She would pick up anything from nature on the playground that she found. That didn't bother me. It was when she began bringing it all in the classroom and playing with it during class that brought on "nature stays outside". She needed to be reminded almost every day. She would bring me a worm she found on the playground and I would just tell her that's nice, but nature stays outside.

Psalm 95:4-5 - In His hands are the depths of the earth, and the mountain peaks belong to Him. The sea is His, for He made it, and His hands form the dry land.

It's important to remember that God made all of nature for us to enjoy. When you are outside, look around and enjoy the beauty that God created: the mountains, the sea, the land. Look at the nature with childlike amazement and thank God for the beauty He has given us. Find beauty in the ants, the worms, the weeds. God made it all.

I'm not saying you have to bring nature inside, but at least enjoy it outside.

Dear God, Thank you for the beautiful nature that you created. Help me to see it with childlike amazement. Amen

Day 18

Bugs! Bugs! Bugs!

Lice, bed bugs, flies, ants, even fleas have made an appearance in classrooms over the years. Sometimes they ride in on the students and sometimes they are carried in by the students (remember nature stays outside). Bugs don't normally give me the creeps, but the thought of lice will always make me scratch my head. You are probably scratching yours right now also! Left unchecked bugs can spread very quickly.

Galatians 5:17 - For the sinful nature desires what is contrary to the Spirit, and the Spirit what is contrary to the sinful nature. They are in conflict with each other, so that you do not do what you want.

Sin left unchecked can also spread very quickly. Everyone struggles with different things, but we all have a sinful nature. That sinful nature wants something different than what God wants for us. Sin will distract us from following what God wants us to do. It can get out of hand very quickly. Everyone sins and makes mistakes; but it is important to not let it grow out of control. Bring it to God and acknowledge it, don't try to hide it.

Don't allow you sin to be like lice or bed bugs and spread. Get it under control and ask God for forgiveness as soon as possible!

Dear God, Please forgive me for the sin in my life. Help me to acknowledge when I've done something wrong and bring it to you. Amen

Day 19

"Don't run in the hall."

Why is it that as soon as no teacher is looking, kids want to run down the hallway? When I was a kid, I would take as long as I could on an errand. Now they can't wait to get to where they are going.

Hebrews 12:1-2 – Therefore, since we are surrounded by such a great cloud of witnesses, let us throw off everything that hinders and the sin that so easily entangles. And let us run with perseverance the race marked out for us, fixing our eyes on Jesus, the pioneer and perfecter of faith. For the joy set before him he endured the cross, scorning its shame, and sat down at the right hand of the throne of God.

The author of Hebrews is speaking of the people in the Bible who displayed great faith when he speaks of the "cloud of witnesses". We are to throw off anything that is hindering us in our walk with God and expel any sin that we are aware of in our lives, so we can "run" for Jesus! Each of us has our own race marked for us in our lives. We should each do our best to discover it and run it with "perseverance" and keep our eyes on Jesus.

Run like the kids in the hallway when no one is watching; the only difference being that you want people to see you be successful in running your race for God.

Dear God, Help me to run my race in a way that shows the world that I am yours. Help me to run like no one is watching but you! Amen

Day 20

"Are you sitting?" "Where are you sitting?" "Are you making good choices about where you are sitting?"

Sometimes we ask kids silly questions to see if they are paying attention. As teachers we know which children should not sit by each other. We try to avoid problems by strategically seating children. Sometimes we allow them to choose where they sit. Who do they choose to sit beside? Where do they choose to sit?

Where are we "sitting" in our Christian walk?

Psalm 1:1 – "Blessed is the man who does not walk in the counsel of the wicked or stand in the way of sinners or sit in the seat of mockers."

Psalm 26:5 – "I abhor the assembly of evildoers and refuse to sit with the wicked."

Ephesians 2:6 – "And God raised us up with Christ and seated us with him in the heavenly realms of Christ Jesus"

We need to make sure that we are reaching out to the unbelievers and showing them Jesus. However, that does not mean we need to *sit* with them. Sitting implies that you are going to stay where they are. As a Christian we are not to sit and stay in sin or wickedness. We are to be raised up and seated with God.

Where are you sitting? Are you making good choices about who you are sitting with?

Dear God, Help me to sit with Jesus. Help me to make good choices about who I am with. Amen

Day 21

"Walk!"

This is a statement heard many times in an elementary school. Mostly called after a child has run or jogged past a teacher in the hallway. The kids know they are supposed to walk. That doesn't stop many of them from trying to run anyway.

Mark 2:9-11 - Which is easier: to say to the paralytic, 'Your sins are forgiven,' or to say, 'Get up, take your mat, and walk?' But that you may know that the Son of Man has authority on earth to forgive sins... He said to the paralytic, "I tell you, get up, take your mat, and go home.

Jesus did many miracles that are recorded in the Bible. This is just one of them. He told a man that couldn't walk to get up and walk! And what's even crazier is that he did! He also told the man that his sins were forgiven. He did this to show that He has the power to forgive sins as well as perform miracles. If Jesus has the power to make men walk, make men see, bring people back to life, feed thousands, and on; then do not doubt Him when He says He has the power to forgive our sins!

So walk! And follow Jesus!

Dear Lord, Thank you for the miracles that are recorded in the Bible. Thank you for your forgiveness! Help me to never take it for granted. Amen

Day 22

"Mom"

How often do I get called "Mom"? At least once a week. I've even been called Dad! No matter what type of home life a child comes from; school and their teacher are a constant for them. God is our constant. No matter what situation we come from, God is always there. If you had an amazing father who modeled what a father should be; God is even better. If you had a father who was a horrible role model or no father; God is there to be your father. Let God be your constant and show you a father's love.

1 John 3:1 – See what great love the Father has lavished on us, that we should be called children of God! And that is what we are! The reason the world does not know us is that it did not know him.

God lavishes his love on us. Imagine yourself a cup and God the pitcher pouring so much love (water) into your cup that it constantly overflows. He never stops pouring His love into you. Even when it doesn't feel like it, He never stops loving you. Sometimes, we just need to stop what we are trying to do and let Him.

God is our Father and our constant!

Dear Lord, Help me to remember that I am a child of God and my students are children of God. You love us more than I can imagine. Thank you! Amen

Day 23

"My kids"

If I have ever taught you; you are forever one of "my kids". Every teacher I know refers to their class as "my kids". When I talk about "my kids" I always have to specify if they are "my school kids" or "my personal kids". It can get a bit confusing at times. I love every single child that I have ever taught and each one will always have a special place in my heart.

Ephesians 1:4-5 – For he chose us in him before the creation of the world to be holy and blameless in his sight. In love he predestined us for adoption to sonship through Jesus Christ, in accordance with his pleasure and will-

God looks at us as "His kids". His ultimate plan is that we all be "adopted" into His family so that we will all end up in Heaven with Him. This is a choice that each person must make on their own and accept God's love. It is a gift. None of us is holy and blameless on our own; we can only strive to be.

There is nothing you or I can do to make God love us any less. He loves you more than anyone possibly can. Let Him be your "adopted" Father today! We are all God's kids!

Dear God, Thank you for allowing me to be your child. Help me to live in accordance with your will. Amen

Day 24

"Can't you just be nice and give me the answers!"

When a child doesn't know the answer right away, they just want someone to give it to them. Sometimes it feels mean when someone won't just give you the answers. Is it really mean or is it a learning experience? I'm not going to use a specific piece of scripture for this. I'm going to refer to the entire Bible!

There is a big push right now for students to go back into the text to find their answers. There are three types of questions in reading: right there questions, using a few different parts of the text questions, and inferring questions (using the text and what you already know). For any question, it is relatively simple for a child to go back and look for the answer.

The Bible holds all our answers.

It would be much easier if someone just told us all the answers. The Bible does that. Some answers are there in black and white. Some answers, you may have to use different scriptures to find your answer. Sometimes you may have to use the Bible and what you already know to find your answer.

God has already given us all the answers. We just have to use our resources and find the answer.

Dear Lord, Help me to remember that all the answers I need are in your word. You have already given them to me, I just need to look. Thank you! Amen

Day 25

"Put your name on your paper"

It is so difficult to get some students to put their names on their papers. When you have several students who don't do this, it can be impossible to tell what paper belongs to which student. Teacher's become experts at deciphering handwriting and drawings; but the multiple choice papers are really impossible to tell apart. There have been many times I pull a few students back to my desk and ask them which paper belongs to them.

Isaiah 43:1b - Fear not, for I have redeemed you; I have summoned you by name; you are mine.

God knows you by name!

That should be the most comforting thing you've heard. Even when you forget who you are; God knows. Even when you struggle with finding yourself; God knows. Even when you can't see your next step; God knows. He knows you and He sees you. He knows who you are! He cares about you! He has redeemed us and called us by name!

If you forgot to put your name on something, God would know it was yours. He doesn't even need you to put your name on your paper!

Dear God, Thank you for knowing me in a way that only you can. Thank you for caring about me and redeeming me. Thank you for calling me yours! Amen

Day 26

Work with your partner

Partner work is so important in schools. They can talk through things, learn from each other, bounce ideas off of each other, etc. When I put students with their partners, it's because I want to see their ideas and see them work through problems together. Sometimes they are still very unsure of themselves and look to me for support instead of looking to their partner. Usually by the end of a school year they are very good at working with their partner. I am still there for the hard parts and can provide guidance and clarification when needed, but they are better able to monitor themselves.

*Matthew 18:20 - **For where two or three gather in My name, there am I with them.***

As Christians we also need to learn to work with our partners (brothers and sisters in Christ). We can lean on one another and work together to show others God's love. Sometimes it may be scary to step out and work with others, but God gave us the promise that if we gather in His name (even with only one or two other people) He is there too. He is there for the hard parts, guidance, and clarification when we need it. But the more we work with other Christians, the easier it is and the better we get at it.

We need to work with the partners God has given us and work to the best of our abilities for His kingdom.

Dear God, Help me to work with the people you have put into my life to further your kingdom. Amen

Day 27

What do you want to be when you grow up?

The age old question that we ask children. I ask my own children at home and my kids at school. Some of them have no idea, some have a clear and direct plan, and some have very far-fetched ideas. I wanted to be in the WNBA when I was young (I'm 5'5"). We should encourage children to have dreams and hopes for their future. They need to know that with hard work and dedication, they can do whatever they set their minds to.

Jeremiah 29:11 - For I know that plans I have for you, declares the Lord. Plans to prosper you and not to harm you; plans to give you a hope and a future.

God has plans for us. He wants us to succeed, have great hope and a wonderful future. This doesn't mean that there won't be tough times; it just means that He will be there to see us through them. It also means that no matter what we choose to do or be in life; God has plans for us to be successful. No one ever asks adults what they want to be when they grow up.

So, what do you want to be? We should want to be a child of God. And we should want to please the Lord in all that we do.

Dear Lord, Let me remember that you have a plan for me; plans to prosper me, not cause me harm. Plans to give me hope and a future. Help me to live a life that is pleasing to you and to serve you in all that I do. Amen

Day 28

"Don't lick your shoes."

"Don't pick your nose."

"Don't eat paper clips."

There are lots of "don't do these things" in schools and life in general. Most of the time in life people don't need to be reminded to not lick their shoes and not to eat paper clips. However sometimes we all need reminders. This reminds me a lot of a "Thou Shalt Not" list in the bible.

Thou shalt not...

1. *Have any other gods before me*
2. *Make for yourself any idol...*
3. *Misuse the name of the Lord your God*
4. *You should remember the Sabbath day*
5. *You should honor your father and mother*
6. *Murder*
7. *Commit adultery*
8. *Steal*
9. *Give false testimony against your neighbor*
10. *Covet your neighbor's house...*

Many times we have to remind students of what they shouldn't do, just as God had to remind the Israelites and us what we shouldn't do. "Don't eat paper clips" should be common sense, but sometimes people need to be told common sense things for them to sink in. "Do not murder, steal, commit adultery, etc." should all be common sense, but God still found that people need to be told.

Have some common sense and follow God's rules. Most of it is as easy as "Don't lick your shoes! Don't pick your nose! Don't eat paper clips!"

Dear God, Help me to remember and follow your rules. They are not hard to follow. Amen

Day 29

"How old is your brother?"

"5 pounds, 6 ounces!"

I was asking one of my new students about his family. He said he had a brother, so I asked how old the brother was. Turns out he just had a new baby brother and misunderstood what I was asking. Thinking about age and understanding look at this verse:

Job 36:26 – How great is God – beyond our understanding! The number of his years is past finding out.

God is greater beyond what we can even understand! That makes me feel safe and secure. Even when I don't understand what He is doing in my life, He is in control. He can do more than we can ever imagine or understand.

Also it says in regards to the age old question "How old is God?" – "the number of his years is past finding out." That's incredible because mathematicians and scientists have the ability to count to a number higher than any stretch of my imagination! God is even older than that! He has always been here and will always be here. Even though that thought seems unfathomable for us to understand it is comforting. There is nothing that can happen that He hasn't already seen and cannot solve. He is always working things out in His timing.

Remember God is beyond our understanding, even when we don't understand.

Dear Lord, Help me to remember that you are in control of every situation that arises in my life and the lives of my students. Help me to remember that you will work all things out for your good. Amen

Day 30

We don't chew the gum you find under the table

Sometimes we don't think of the consequences of what we are doing. A kid finds a piece of gum and chews it. That's ok most of the time; just not when it's already been chewed. We discourage chewing gum in schools, because at some point a child will pick up a chewed piece and eat it.

1 Corinthians 10:23 - Everything is permissible - but not everything is beneficial. Everything is permissible - but not everything is constructive.

God gave us free will. If we want to chew the gum we found under the table we can - but it's not beneficial. Just because everything is permissible, does not mean it's beneficial or constructive. Our society has become very ego-centric. If it feels good, do it. We are allowed to choose for ourselves what to do and what not to do. However, it is important to remember that not everything is beneficial or constructive. When we keep God in the forefront of our minds and the center of our lives, it is easier to see what is beneficial and constructive.

If you really want to chew the used gum, you can; but is it what is best for you?

Dear Lord, Help me to use my free will that you have so graciously given to me in a good way. Help me to make good choices, keeping you in mind in all that I do. Amen

Day 31

Tape is not for eating. Only food goes in your mouth

Sometimes it does make you wonder why certain things even need to be said. There are so many wonderful and different foods that exist for us to eat. Yet little kids insist on putting other things into their mouths. Tape, fuzz, anything they find on the floor; they will put it in their mouths.

*Genesis 2:16-17 - **And the Lord God commanded the man, "You are free to eat from any tree in the garden; but you must not eat from the tree of the knowledge of good and evil, for when you eat of it you will surely die."***

God told Adam not to eat from one tree in the garden. He could eat of any of the many other trees.

Genesis 3:11b - Have you eaten from the tree that I commanded you not to eat from?

Of course, Adam and Eve are just like children who choose to put anything but food into their mouths. They had many other choices and only one thing they weren't supposed to eat. They did it anyway.

There are many things that we do, even though we know we shouldn't. God has given us many amazing things that we can and should do. Yet, we still make bad decisions.

Eat your food and follow God's directions!

Dear God, Help me to follow your directions. Let me be a good role model for my students. Amen

Day 32

We don't eat our clothes.

Some kids like to chew on their clothes. They either chew on the neck, stretching it out or chew on their sleeves if they have long sleeves on. Sometimes their shirts become soaked with their saliva. Through different training I've been in I have learned that this is called an oral fixation and that some students need to have something in their mouth in order to focus. However, I do try to convince them not to eat their clothes and work on finding something more appropriate to keep their focus.

*Proverbs 4:27 - **Do not turn to the right or to the left; turn your foot from evil.***

As Christian's we sometimes have trouble keeping our focus on God also. There are many reminders throughout the bible about keeping our focus on God. I like the verse above from Proverbs. There are so many things in life that can take our focus away from God: sin, fun, family, TV, phones, work, school, pets, friends, etc. Not all of these things are bad things, but can distract us if we allow them. This verse reminds us to stay on the path God wants us on and not to veer to the right or the left. It also reminds us to stay away from evil.

Find what helps you keep your focus on God and go with it. I just hope it's not chewing on your shirt!

Dear Lord, Please help me to stay focused on You and the path You want me on. Do not allow me to become distracted; but when I do, help me to turn away from the distractions and focus back on You. Amen

Day 33

Stop stroking my foot

I had a student once who would rub my foot. Every time we were on the carpet he would try to sit in front of me so he could rub my foot. He was a chatty one, so I inevitably would place him in the front near me so I could keep the talking in check. I would try to ignore the foot stroking, but I would eventually have to tell him to stop. He would tell me that my shoes were soft and pretty.

Isaiah 52:7 - How beautiful on the mountains are the feet of those who bring good news, who proclaim peace, who bring good tidings, who proclaim salvation, who say to Zion, "Your God reigns!"

I want God to say that I have beautiful feet! I want to be the one who brings the good news of Jesus to people! I know in public schools we are very limited in what we are allowed to say and do in regards to religion. But we can still love the kids in our classrooms the way Jesus does. Some of them have never heard of Jesus before. We can show them His love.

We can also be active in other ways in bringing the good news to people. It can start with our own families, churches, towns, communities, etc. Be involved, teach in church, pray for your community, People will know that you are a believer by your actions and your love for others.

Be someone that God says has beautiful feet. Have such beautiful feet that people want to "stroke them".

Dear God, Give me beautiful feet as I bring the Good News to people who haven't heard. Let me be a light to the people around me, so they will see you! Amen

Day 34

Please turn off your shoes

Who decided it was a good idea to make shoes light up with a button? When kids wear them, that's all they want to do is play with the button and turn their shoes on and off. That makes all the other kids in class look at their shoes. And for some reason, the shoes become the most fascinating thing they've ever seen. They are more enthralled with shoes than with what is being taught. To get them to pay attention, you have to tell them to turn off the shoes. Only then can they focus on what is being taught.

Proverbs 4:1 - Listen, my sons, to a father's instruction, pay attention and gain understanding.

Proverbs 4:20 - My son, pay attention to what I say; listen closely to my words.

We also need to pay attention to the important things. So often we allow distractions into our lives, like light up shoes. Distractions can come in so many forms; anything that keeps our attention from God is a distraction. They don't even have to be bad things. It is important to keep Jesus at the center of anything you are doing. These verses are just two of many examples where God's words instruct us to pay attention and listen. If you pay attention and listen to what God says; you will gain understanding, wisdom and so much more!

Turn off your shoes and focus on God.

Dear Lord, Help me not to be distracted by the things in my life. Help me to keep you in the center of my life. Amen

Day 35

Does that ring a bell?

Do you understand?

Sometimes teachers can get frustrated when they know that the kids have already learned something. After I give directions I always ask if they understand what I just said and ask if anyone has questions. I have heard teachers also ask if that rings a bell for kids. We just need to know that kids acknowledge what we've said and understood it.

Proverbs 3:5-6 - Trust in the Lord with all your heart and lean not on your own understanding; in all your ways acknowledge him and he will make your paths straight.

When asked what my favorite verse is, I always say this one. It has always reminded me that no matter what I think or what the devil may be trying to whisper in my ear, that I cannot always trust my understanding of things. I need to trust in the Lord. He will remind me of the promises He has given me and show me where I need to go. God just wants to make sure we understand what He has said and have us acknowledge that we understand it.

Does that ring a bell? Do we understand?

Dear God, Help me to trust in you with all that I am. Help me to understand what you want for me and lead me in the direction you want me to go. Amen

Day 36

Write it, don't say it

I usually have a writing prompt every day for students to practice writing about something specific. Sometimes they get so excited that they just have to share it with everyone around them. I always tell them that their writing time is silent time. Then I give them time to share them at the end. I have to say many times that they need to write it and not talk about it. I want them to get their thoughts down on paper first.

Proverbs 7:3 - Bind them on your fingers; write them on the tablet of your heart.

This verse specifically speaks about the commands from Proverbs. If we are to write something on the tablet of our hearts, that means we should know it completely, follow and use it. In order to write a command or proverb on our hearts that also means that we need to study it. It's easy to read the bible and check it off your list of things to do. What we need to do though is really study it so we know it by heart. Then we are better able to share our faith with others.

Use your bible study time to focus and be silent to study and listen to God. Write it on your heart first so you can talk about it later.

Dear Lord, Help me to study your word and write it on my heart. Then I can share it with others. Amen

Day 37

Reread the directions

Sometimes I feel like I say this a lot! Even as an adult I struggle with reading all the directions on something. I may glance at the directions and think I know what I am doing, only to find out halfway through that I really didn't. Kids need many reminders about reading directions. I can always tell when grading papers who actually read the directions. Sometimes even when I read the directions out loud some still have to reread them.

James 2:23-25 - Anyone who listens to the word but does not do what it says is like a man who looks at his face in a mirror and after looking at himself goes away and immediately forgets what he looks like. But the man who looks intently into the perfect law that gives freedom, and continues to do this not forgetting what he has heard, but doing it - he will be blessed in what he does.

The bible is there with all the directions we need in life. We just have to read, reread, and actually follow the directions the Lord has placed there for us. Sometimes we've read the directions but choose not to follow them. But there is also a blessing tied into following God's perfect law.

Pay attention to God's directions and when you forget, go back and reread the directions.

Dear God, Help me to follow the directions you have given us. Help me to not just read it, but to do what you say. Amen

Day 38

Make good choices

I remind my students to make good choices daily. Make good choices about where you are sitting, when you are talking, what you are focusing on, how hard you are working, etc. If kids learn at a young age that they are responsible for making their own choices and that they are capable of making good choices, they are more likely to make good choices in the future.

Joshua 24:15 (ESV) - And if it is evil in your eyes to serve the Lord, choose this day whom you will serve, whether the gods your fathers served in the region beyond the River, or the gods of the Amorites in whose land you dwell. But as for me and my house, we will serve the Lord.

As adults there are many choices we have to make every day (approximately 35,000 versus a child's 3,000). Some are more important than others. What shirt I wear is probably not as significant as the way I choose to speak to others. All of our decisions pale in comparison to the biggest choice we ever make, serving the Lord. There are so many things in the world to choose from: different religions, self, no religion, etc. We need to make the greatest choice: following and serving the Lord. This is a choice that you have to make every day; to serve the Lord and follow Him.

Remember daily: make good choices; serve the Lord.

Dear Lord, Help me to choose every day to serve You. Help me make good choices to follow You. Amen

Day 39

Use kind words

We all need a reminder on this once in a while. I spend time talking to the kids in my classes about using kind words with each other and being respectful to each other. I also do a lot of discussion about tone of voice. That you might not be saying anything mean, but the tone of your voice is mean. Use kind words and use a kind tone with everyone you interact with.

Ephesians 4:32 - Be kind and compassionate to one another, forgiving each other, just as in Christ God forgave you.

As Christian's God wants us to be not just kind to everyone, but to show each other compassion also. Also, we are to forgive each other when someone isn't kind or doesn't show compassion to us. We are supposed to do all of this because God forgave us. No matter what we have done in our lives, how bad it is, God will forgive us.

We need to show God's love to everyone around us, so they will understand how much God loves them.

Use kind words!

Dear God, Help me to use kind words today and every day. Help me to show others your kindness and compassion. Help me also to forgive others, the way you have forgiven me. Amen

Day 40

The words are not on my face. You aren't actually reading if you aren't looking at the words.

Reading together as a class is always an interesting event. You have students who try to speed read and stay ahead of everyone. You have kids who don't even try to read. You have kids who read with you. And you have kids who look at the teacher the entire time while "reading". Many times I have to remind students that in order to read, they actually have to look at the words on the page. Those words are not on my face, so if they are looking at me they aren't actually reading.

Psalm 119:11 - I have hidden your word in my heart, that I might not sin against you.

This verse is what we should all aspire to. I want to read God's word and study it to the point that I have it in my heart to recall anytime I want. Then I won't even have to read it, I will be able to recite it. When I was a kid, I was in a church program that promoted memorizing scripture. The verses I learned as a child, I still can mostly quote today. It is much harder to memorize things as an adult, but I still try.

Study and memorize scripture so it is in your heart. Then you won't need to look at the words to "read" it. It will be in your head to recall whenever you need it.

Dear God, Help me to study and hide your word in my heart. Then I can use it at all times! Amen

Day 41

I don't do "what ifs".

Kids are really good at what iffing. What if the fire alarm goes off, what if I lose my shoe, what if we get a new student, what if a mouse runs through the room, what if I get sick, what if I throw up on my paper, etc. Sometimes I will give them a real answer; if they ask about the fire alarm, I will tell them what we would do. Sometimes their what ifs are very over the top or just continue on and on with different scenarios. I always respond then with "I don't do what ifs. I deal with what is." Then we take a minute to discuss what is actually happening.

Adults do this with a lot of things also. If you don't reign it in and give the what ifs to God, they can overwhelm you.

Matthew 6:34 - Therefore do not worry about tomorrow, for tomorrow will worry about itself. Each day has enough trouble of its own.

What ifs are really just worries that are non-existent. What ifs are worries that we make up that usually do not happen anyway. That's why God tells us not to worry (especially about things that might not happen. Each day gives you enough worries of its own. You don't need to make more of them up. Trust that God will take care of everything each day and give up your worries.

What if I throw up on my paper? What if you don't? Don't invent what ifs. Trust God.

Dear God, Help me to trust you with my what ifs. Help me to let go of my what ifs and trust you to take care of all my worries. Amen

Day 42

"My crayon's broken! I can't use it anymore."

My response is always, "Broken crayons still color." Perspective changes things. When you are a child you think that if a crayon is broken, it can't possibly work. As you get older and you realize how many crayons students will go through if you replace every broken crayon; you understand that broken crayons work just fine. They may not be as pretty on the outside, but the color in them works just as well as a brand new crayon. Being broken isn't necessarily a bad thing.

Psalm 51:17 – My sacrifice, O God, is a broken spirit; a broken and contrite heart you, God, will not despise.

David sinned over and over again, yet God called him a man after God's own heart. That is because David came to God with a "broken and contrite heart". David was broken, humble, grieving, and crushed by his sins. When we come to God crushed and broken by our sins; only then can God mold us in the way He wants us. God is pleased when we come to Him with a broken heart, because He can use you to your fullest then. If we give God our broken heart, He will not despise it. More than that; He will love it! It is when we are broken and realize we need God that we can truly shine.

Broken people can still be used for God's glory – just like broken crayons can still be used to color.

Dear Lord, So many students have come to me feeling broken. Help them to know that broken people can be used for God's glory. Amen

Day 43

It's ok to make a mistake, but it's not ok to leave it a mistake.

One of my biggest pet peeves as a teacher is when you ask a student to fix something on a paper before they turn it in and they don't do it. I have many discussions with every class I've had about making mistakes. Everyone makes mistakes and it's ok to make mistakes because that's how we learn. However, if you know it's a mistake then it's not ok to leave it a mistake. If I have told a student for example that 2+2 does not equal the 5 that they have written down and they don't attempt to change it before they turn it in; that is not ok.

Romans 10:9-10 - That if you confess with your mouth, "Jesus is Lord, and believe in your heart that God raised him from the dead, you will be saved. For it is with your heart that you believe and are justified, and it is with your mouth that you confess and are saved.

Everyone makes mistakes. The important thing is to admit that you've made mistakes and change them. Believe in your heart that Jesus died on the cross and God raised him from the dead and confess it with your mouth; you will be saved. We will always make mistakes because only Jesus was perfect. It's important to admit you've made a mistake and do your best to change it. Fix your mistakes.

It's ok to make a mistake, but it's not ok to leave it a mistake.

Dear Lord, Help me to remember that we all make mistakes. Help me to fix the mistakes that I have made and do my best not to make the same mistakes again. Amen

Day 44

It's not hard, it just takes time.

I say this all the time; when students are tasked with a test, a written response, a word problem, or anything else they perceive as hard. Most of the time what they see as hard isn't really hard, it's just something that will take them time to work through. That "hard" word problem is really just a multiple step addition and multiplication problem. They can add and multiply, it's just going to take them some time to work it out. That hard written response question; the answer is actually right there in the text. It will just take them some time to craft a well written response.

Knowing and following God's will isn't hard, but it does take time.

1 John 5:3 - *This is love for God: to obey his commands. And his commands are not burdensome,*

If we love God, we can show others that love by obeying his commands. His greatest command is to love one another. It also states that his commands are not burdensome or hard. Sometimes it feels hard to follow God and his commands. Is it really hard though or does it just take some time? The more time you spend with God through prayer and the bible; the more you will see that it's not hard to follow God's will and commands. The less time we spend with God the more difficult or burdensome it will seem. Spend time with God and show love to other people!

It's not hard to love others and to follow God; it just takes some time and effort.

Dear God, Help me to take the time to follow you and to love others in the way you want me to. Amen

Day 45

Everybody farts

It's very rare that you make it through a full day of school without some nosy bodily function coming from a student. And without a doubt one or more of those students will then snicker about it. That then inevitably leads at some point to the comment that "everybody farts"; many times leading to more snickering. However, it is true!

Romans 3:23 - for all have sinned and fall short of the glory of God,

This verse clearly tells us that "everybody sins". No one is perfect and we all fall short of earning our way to heaven. Which is why God sent His son. I believe that there are many times that one verse can speak volumes and get a fantastic point across, this verse included. However, we cannot discount taking those same verses and reading around them for a bit more context.

Romans 3:22, 24-25a - This righteousness from God comes through faith in Jesus Christ to ALL who BELIEVE. There is no difference (v. 23); and are JUSTIFIED freely by his GRACE through the redemption that came by Christ Jesus. God presented him as a sacrifice of atonement, through faith in his blood. (emphasis mine)

Romans 3:23 on it's own is a very powerful verse that reminds us that no one is perfect and on our own cannot get to heaven. The verses surrounding it bring to light the HOW we can get to heaven. That anyone can be justified by our belief in Jesus because of his blood. We cannot earn it because of our sin. But Jesus died for all of us!

So remember: everybody farts, everyone sins, but Jesus died for all to go to heaven!

Dear God, Thank you for sending Jesus for sinners like me. Everyone has sinned, help me to focus on living out my faith so others can see Jesus in me. Amen

Katie has been an elementary school teacher for 14 years teaching Reading Intervention, 1st Grade, 3rd Grade, and 5th Grade. Katie has been a Pastor's daughter for her whole life. She lives in the mountains of Maryland with her husband and two children.

Made in the USA
Las Vegas, NV
19 August 2021